Write Our Wrongs

A Victims Impact Iniative

Created by Donel Poston and James Wilson in High Desert State Prison

Preface

I "met" James 10+ years ago as pen-pals and we have been steadfast friends since. I met Donel only few years ago when James was serving as the coordinator of a prison, anger-management correspondence-course and he had asked Donel to join the group.

I am honored to have been asked to write this preface. (This book was truly complete without the addition of any of my words.)

Let me share with you a quote James and I have batted back and forth over the years:

> The difference between a prison and a monastery is a matter of perspective.

Donel and James are two monks of the High Desert Correctional Monastery of Susanville, CA. They have each confronted who they were, decided to change, and have transformed their lives. (How many folk do you know who do that?)

Moreover, they have chosen to share their light with as many as they can. That's the point of this book — to share honestly about the truths that they and others have found.

I hope you and thousands more are inspired to find the grace to transform. I am certain no matter your religious affiliation your life will be blessed for having read these words.

With love,

-Rabbi Brian Zachary Mayer

Introduction

Mother Theresa once said, "No one can do great things, they can only do small things with love."

This small project is one of those things, humble work, undertaken with love. No, it is not a perfect project but it comes from the growing hearts of men who once could do wrong with impunity. So it took great courage for all of us to write the contents of this book.

Please do not hold us to the standard of those worthy men who have found total redemption, for we are still glasses half empty. We see imperfectly.

Much of the inspiration for this project owes itself to many other people, above all, Shaka Senghor, the author of <u>Writing My Wrongs</u> who has become a must read in our circle of friends. The Ear Hustle Podcast crew (Earlonne Woods, Nigel Poor, et al) deserves a shot out, too!

We owe little to ourselves. Keeping with that spirit none of the proceeds for this book will go to any inmate involved with this project. All monies earned will go to a Victims Impact Fund.

We are thankful for all the assistance from everyone who made this project possible, including the High Desert State Prison Administration and Tajai Massey.

We are deeply indebt.

Inmates at High Desert State Prison

About Donel Poston

(Cofounder of Write Our Wrongs Project)

A life of destructive living only lands you in two places: a prison cell or a coffin. Well, I've been near death a time or two and I've had my ample share of cell living; throughout that time I never wanted to be accountable for the crimes that I've committed and the human beings that I have hurt.

Presently, I am confined to a cell for a life sentence, but through projects like this I have been given an opportunity at repentance. Rightfully, I have accepted my sentence because society is owed reparations for the crimes I have committed. More so, this is a rebirth and a chance to reinvent myself. First, I have actively began to cleanse my soul. Next, I have rewired my thinking. And currently, I'm making a conscious effort at being selfless.

On my recent journey I have cofounded several self-help groups, earned two degrees, and written three books. Alongside Write Our Wrongs, the self-help groups co-founded with James Wilson are operating (New Hearts and Reaching Out From Within), as well as Choices, co-founded with Brian Fiore.

The only way that I can come to grips with all the harm I have caused is to begin giving back to the countless number of victims that I've created. Write Our Wrongs has allowed me to evolve into the next stage of compensating my victims. This project is a sincere effort, by prisoners like myself, to return a modicum of monetary support for all the families and victims that we have created in our lifetime.

I am very grateful for all the people who have helped me reach this place and given me inspiration on my journey to finding myself:
Allah, Leatta Poston, Bobby Turner, Tajai Massey and Hieroglyphics, Miangle Cody and Brittany K. Barnette (Buried Alive Project), The Incarcerated Collective, Bryan Stevenson, Meek Mill, Jay-Z, Charlamagne Tha God, and all the people who are actively working on prison reform. Most importantly, thank you to all the

participants that bared their soul in an effort to make amends for all the wrongs they have done. Mr. Shaka Senghor, thank you for giving us a pick to help us unlock these human cages.

About James Wilson
(Cofounder of Write Our Wrongs Project)

There are some people who belong in prison and I am one of them. The streets wanted me dead; the cops and my victims families wanted me on death row, hoping the state would kill me via lethal injection some day.

During 15 years of incarceration I have sought to redeem my soul and justify my reason for being, fully embracing the mercy - the undeserved kindness - God has granted me.

Seeking to express contrition in action turned me to prayer, meditation, profusive reading, writing literature, and mentoring other men in the prison community, mostly through self-help groups. I've co-founded (T.R.Y and The Self-Improvement class).

This current project, Write Our Wrongs, is one of several recent projects I have worked on with Donel Poston. The other projects have been transformed into self-help groups and are currently operating (New H.E.A.R.T.S and Reaching Out From Within). All of this information is on the website "prisonsfoundation.com". Jason Howard, whose story is included in this book, is working with Donel and myself to establish an inter-faith class to initiate dialogue and brotherhood within the religious community in prison. Service is paying my rent for the space I occupy on this Earth. I would be remissed in my duty if I diddn't mention the biggest inspirations in my life at this point: Nate Williams, Karen McDaniels Daniel "Nagy" Buckley Jr., Jane Mayer, Rabbi Brian Mayer, Robin Shanker, Alex Taylor Carmelo Duca, Van Jones, Kim Kardahian, and more. None other than the author of Writing My Wrongs, Shaka Senghor, and all the men who took the brave step to write their stories for this book project - without all of you this book would not have been possible. God is in the midst.

Gabriel Weston

In Retrospect

If I knew what I knew now back before I caught this case, I would have held my family tight to my chest. I would have noticed all the support I had around me, all the _true_ friendships that just wanted the best for me.

I would have taken my sobriety as a life or no life factor; that there is no half-stepping sobriety, that I could never love someone fully if I couldn't love and care for myself.

I would have seen all the fake people I chose to surround myself with. I would have been able to spot the lies and the weightless words, all the valuable time wasted.

I must say this on the reality side of things, my growth as a man has been a total tranformation of who I once was. I have been able to feel how tender life is, how precious family is. I am a strong Muslim man that only found Islam by this result of my old ways. In this past chapter of my life I have been blessed to meet and build a crazy strong relationship with my biological family, that drowns me in love. I am an older brother to three little girls and a boy, and God has blessed me two mothers.

I wouldn't change anything because of all the progress I've made and the progress that I'm still making every year.

Gabriel Weston
AS-1208

Lamont J. Howard

The Next Time

I am the manifestation of my next time.

My next time will be full of integrity, honesty, and hard work.

My next time is right now!

Lamont J. Howard
AW-6959

A Letter to My Victims

Being 46 and on this path of becoming a better man; no, learning to be a man there were some things about myself I had to come to terms with. One of the hardest things I had to come to terms with is that I victimized people physically and emotionally. Although I'm truly sorry for the things I've done in my heart, I understand being apologetic is not enough. I know this because it's not enough for me. I also have been victimized and for me the apology didn't repair the damage. But, if I had to ask one thing of the person it would be to change—change your life and never repeat the action again.

So, I promise you I will become a pillar in my community. I will become an influence for positive actions to any one I come in contact with. I promise you if it's in my power I will never allow anyone to become a victim of any circumstance. With this said, although I apologize deeply for the things I have done, I ask deeper for a chance to show you I have changed. I want to become a model, a sincere representative, of the message embodied in this letter. I will be short on words and long on action. Thank you for reading these words.

Lamont J. Howard
AW-6959

In Retrospect

June 6, 1973, was the day of my birth. My first memorable moments of my childhood were living in a house with my mom and dad having lots of toys, family, and friends around. My next memorable moments as a child was a feeling of the world that i knew around me changing. At the age of 10 I felt something pulling my family apart. My dad had been replaced, although he was physically still there. He use to be filléd with love, joy, and fun. My mother had been replaced with sadness and anger; being so young I did not know why I could sense everything had change.

What I didn't know was that the same thing going on in my home and to my family was happening to almost half of my community. My community had been invaded by a soul snatching alien. This invader, this alien, infected millions. My family was among the infected. At first the alien infected my father and the effects of it was the lost of respect in all forms; his familys' well being became of no concern to him. His only purpose in life was to keep the alien happy. I know by now you are wondering what is this alien? Who is this alien? Where did this alien come from? This alien is man made and was designed to destroy. We call it crack cocaine. Crack robbed me of a father and gave my mother anger and heart ache. Our family life stood no chance and the road to every conceivable hardship filled the void of what was once a happy home.

By the age of 12 I realized that this alien didn't just invade communities but created a new paradigm for economic survival, turning young men into drug dealers and potentially good homes into crack houses.

My situation caused me to become frustrated and confused. Being so young and not knowing what to do, I turned angry and so I began to rebel against everyone and anything. It was my only "solution" to the problem.

At the age 13 I became an agent of the invader and began spreading the infection. My young heart had grown calloused and now I was a part of the problem

1

that I despised. I too was infected. By the time I was 26 years old I had turned into an addict myself; not just to a single drug, but to every narcotic I could get my hands on. Moreover, I joined a street gang and became addicted to the street life and the violence that comes with it. After a while I did not recognize my 10 year old self that was happy and easy going. I was an alien, an unknown person, in my own body. I could care less who I hurt. My freedom was even expendable. After serving several terms I found myself back in for 11 years.

Luckily, the light of education and spirituality began to pierce my dark heart. I found that there was still flesh amongst the stone and now I am cultivating that remnant of good and allowing it to grow. Looking back, I know I could never - with my knowledge and experience - become an agent of destruction to myself and my community. Not a day goes by without me lamenting over the hurt and pain I've caused. And everyday I make sure I sew a little more light to push back the darkness that once invaded every thing I understood and knew as right.

In the next chapter of my life I will be an agent for change and community building. I get it.

Lamont J. Howard
AW-6959

Aaron Chandra

The Next Time

What did I do?

Blind to what my actions can cause,
deaf to any voice that tried to help.
Corruption was my fate; destruction and hate,
I took from children, mothers, and friends,
I stole your future and made it end.
How can I make amends? When I took so much,
fatherless children and a widow who's tough.
Who can I blame for the guilt and shame?
The man in the mirror who shares my name.

Next Time

Next time I'll listen,
Next time I'll care,
Next time I'll think,
Next time I'll prepare, so next time is not there.
As these thoughts weigh heavy, I know I'm ready.
I look to the sky and ask for forgiveness,
I ask for wisdom and hope that he listens.
I glorified my actions and showed no compassion,
I laughed at your misery like I did no wrong,
life had no value and my hate was strong.
I can't fight this remorse as I proceed with change,
I pray one day you forgive me and let go of your rage.

Aaron Chandra
AP-0929

A Letter to My Victims

First off, I want to say in no way am I trying to justify my actions. What I did that day was my choice and I am to blame. I hope I can bring some understanding, because in the past I struggled with the significance of my actions and what they caused. I've been able to see that my decisions throughout the course of my life up until my offense led to that action.

However, these choices and decisions created my habits and all compliled in one created my character. My character was selfish, greedy, angry, and full of hatred. I had every opportunity to be the opposite of what I turned into, but I was weak and didn't make the choices that took some strength and discipline. Whatever I was going through at the time, I decided to use drugs and alcohol to help me deal with it, and in the process I had a disregard for anyone, including my family, whose life I risked everyday by selling drugs out of their home. I was a coward becuase I couldn't face my problems as a 19 year old man. I was still a coward at 25 because even then I couldn't face reality and take accountability for what I did.

Furthermore, I've had many days to reflect on the past and I recognize the impact I've had, and how many peoples lives I've hurt and changed forever. I'm so sorry for what I did to you and your three children, stripping you of your family and love one. I can't fathom the pain you felt that day and continue to live with. Knowing that I'm the one who caused all that grief, to all of you, tears me apart, I've prayed to God to never let me become that person again.

I can't continue to search for band-aids or temporary relief for my actions. I need to face them like a man and change myself. Its difficult to change your way of thinking, change your impusive behavior, and change your habits, but it can be done. I'm committed and determined to better myself everyday and I've turned to God for help, strength, and forgiveness. I've learned a lot throughout this process and taking accountability for my actions is a step towards my recovery.

1

I hope you can find the strength to get out of the hole I put you in and per-
severe through everything you face. I will continue to make decisions that lead
to positive actions and allows me to become an overall better human being. I will
help other people avoid my mistakes and make smart decisions to lead them to
successful lives. I struggle with guilt every time my mind drifts to why I'm in
this situation. I deserve every punishment that comes my way, because of the
choices I've made and the damage I've caused to peoples lives. I owe society a
debt, and I hope to one day redeem myself through my actions, so the person that
I was will be unrecognizable to me and others who know me.

Aaron Chandra
AP-0929

In Retrospect

If I knew then what I know now, I wouldn't resort to violence to solve a problem. I understand that conflict will occur throughout the course of living, but the way you handle those situations shouldn't be violent. Growing up and maturing, I realize all my faults and the mistakes I've made because of my choices. What I know now is to be considerate of others and don't be selfish or self-centered.

I would be aware of all the lives I could alter with my actions and stay away from situations that can have these outcomes. I would've listened to that voice in my conscience instead of reacting impulsively. I would've surrounded myself with different individuals who were headed in another direction. If I knew then what I know now, there wouldn't be a victim because of my actions. I wouldn't be capable of causing pain to so many people.

If I knew then what I know now, they wouldn't feel the way they do, I wouldn't feel like this, and none of this would've happened. I was raised by a loving family who still supports me till this day. My mom always provided all the necessities for me and my two siblings, but I took all that for granted. A single parent couldn't do a better job at raising three children on their own like she did. I started living a life of deceit fueled by pills, alcohol, and marijauna. I let the enemy take over and control my decisions. I turned into something I wasn't with these mind altering substances.

I developed trust issues, anger issues, and other insecurities. I embraced the negative culture I surrounded myself with and became easily influenced by the corruption around me. The world revolved around me, that's how I acted. I ended up turning these issues into resentment, hate, and malice. I ended up taking a mans life. A man who had two children and a wife who was eight months pregnant. How can I make amends for this? I'm 28 years old and I've realized what I've done, I see the monster I was and how many people I've hurt.

1

I ripped a family apart and caused a never ending hardship on so many.

I will, through my actions, do my best to redeem myself and try to help others from making the mistakes I made. Others will see that I've sincerly attempted to right my wrongs to become a the better man my mother tried to raise. I'm so sorry to my victims and anyone I've affected negatively. I hope one day in your heart you can truly forgive me.

Aaron Chandra
AP-0929

Edward (Sababu) Coo

The Next Time

Sentenced to life in prison without the possibilty of parole, plus 7 years,
is indeed a long time,
but at that point in time,
I really didn't mind.
Maybe it was because I was 16 years old at the time,
an thought to myself,
hey,
people commit crimes all the time.
So I told the judge to stop making a big deal out of mine,
an to keep in mind,
that I plan on getting away with mine.
The next time,
an now 25 years later down the line,
the next time is the farthest thing on my mind.
Especially when I call to mind,
all the pain, suffering, trauma, and grime
that comes from commiting crimes of any kind.
An so,
the next time that I see a youngster about to make the same mistakes as mine,
I'll take the time,
to help change their mind about commiting a crime,
an to inform them of the reality of mine,
that their might not be
a next time.

Edward (Sababu) Coo
J-77594

A Letter to My Victims

To my victims, their families, and my community, the words "I'm sorry" do not say enough, you deserve so much more form me than words can convey. I have scribed this correspondence to provide you an opportunity to be witness of my remorse for the pain I have caused you, your family, and my community. I do not presume that you or society want to understand where my heart and my mind are at, but I wanted to provide you, your family, and my community with the opportunity to know my feelings and thoughts. In the 25 years which have passed since I had caused the pain, suffering, and trauma that I am sure your family and my community have had to endure as a result of the senseless brutality at my hands, I have come to accept my actions.

Among the things I have learned, and which prison has given me opportunity is that victims of senseless acts of violence frequently are left with the residue of this violence which causes them to ask why me? why my family? And why in my community? The thoughts and feelings which infest and degrade my own sense of serenity compel me to communicate to you, that this was entirely my fault. While I owe you more than words, at the same time I hope these words provide you and society access to some level of resolution.

At the age of 16, for my crimes, I was sentenced to life in prison without the possibility of parole, plus 7 years. My prison term is deserved. At the same time, the pain it has induced has provided me insight into the pain I have caused you, your family, and my community. I know not if there exist actions I can take which will serve to play a part in healing your family and my community. If your family or members of my community wish to reach out to me for any reason, I promise I will accept whatever they want to convey to me. I am taking advantage of all opportunities to prepare myself to engage in such actions if they exist. I hope the words they find on this page either now or in the future bring some level of relief. For me, I know I would not achieve the best possible

1

version of myself had I not conveyed these words to you and them.

I am reminded on a constant basis of the horrific manner in which I offended you and I can only guess at the ways in which you, your family, and my community have suffered since that night. The fact that I am unable to fully provide myself with an empathic understanding of what I have put you through is both motivation and my own struggle to make amends to you, your family, society, and God. I only wish I could have gained this insight without the pain and disruption I have caused you.

My daily experience is filled with thoughts of regret and remorse for what I have done to you. This regret and remorse guides my commitment to make amends. My commitment to stay on a path consistent with the amends I owe you and society will not be discouraged no matter what level of remorse you and society choose to accept from me. I cannot promise I will never cause hardship to another person, but I can promise you and my community that I will never victimize another person.

I have every intention of respecting societies boundaries. I will not reach out to your family again unless they instruct me to do so. I pray that your family and members of my community will attend my youth parole elgibility hearing, in order to see that my deeds and actions are an example of the fact that, those (like me) who have both suffered and perpetrated the greatest harms also have the greatest capacity for transforming ourselves and our community.

In concluding, I wish for your transcendence from my experience as a victim to your claiming of all the goodness, power, and joy in the afterlife that you are entitled to.

Edward (Sababu) Cook
J-77594

2

In Retrospect

Like all other children I grew up wanting to be the center of attention, not even realizing that the creator will always be the true center of everything.

My story begins with a foundation of drugs, gangs, violence, miseducation, self-hate, and the misuse of religion. Now, for all of us who have lived in the heart of these elements, we know that they are some very powerful things, or should I say that they appear to be very powerful realities when one does not have the knowledge of how to overcome these realities. The Bible and Quran say, "My people are destroyed for a lack of knowledge." I'll begin by stating that I survived the 80s, which was the height of the crack and gang destruction upon the community of people of color and poor white people of America. I played with drugs, however, I had people in my life that prevented me form being able to devote or surrender myself habitually or excessively to them in such a way that would have destroyed me.

Unfortunately, 85% of my community was not so fortunate, I was cursed to witness their destruction. In retrospect, even though I didn't have the best or the strongest support system, I wish that I would have had the knowledge of how to support and guide those around me away from the destruction of drug use. And with that in mind, I now strive to be a good example and I reach out whenever possible an encourage people away from that destructive way of life.

Like most youngsters these days, I was misguided directly into the heart of the gang culture and all of the destruction that comes along with it. In retrospect, I wish that I would have had the knowledge and wisdom of how to communicate and offer that sense of family and community that leads a person to becoming involved in gangs. I now communicate and offer that sense of brotherhood and community to those that are in gangs in order to show them that what they are looking for is able to be had in a life-giving and positive format.

Also, I have survived the violence that is so dominant in this culture.

1

Indeed, like most of the survivors, I understand that the worst violence that one can live through is not physical violence, but emotional violence that destroys the very essence of our being. In retrospect, I now communicate the knowledge, wisdom, and understanding that not only is violence the lowest form of intelligence, but also that violence is like a double edge blade without a handle, which means that violence hurts the person committing the violence and the victim of the violence. This cycle involves miseducation and self-hatred.

An so, I now communicate the knowledge and wisdom that we are all gods, children of the most high God. Because the knowledge of our divine essence and who we are in reality is the first step in loving ourselves, only in loving ourselves will be able to love others. When we love others as we love ourselves then we will not destroy others with acts of violence.

In conclusion, I would like to give all of the youngsters the context in which this letter is being written, but most importantly I want you youngsters to know my aim and purpose for writing this letter to you. That aim and purpose is twofold. One reason is to inform you that I am the big homie that has survived the drugs, gangs, violence, miseducation, self-hate, misuse of religion, and 25 years of level 4 maximum security prison living; 11 of which were spent in the SHU (solitary confinement). But most importantly, my aim and purpose is to give you the knowledge, wisdom, and understanding of my experience so that you will be able to avoid the mistakes that I made. With this knowlege you will gain the courage to start where you stand and begin the journey of self-improvement, which is the basis for community development.

The first step in that journey must be the gaining of knowledge, because once you have the knowledge then you become the master of your situations and circumstances. In retrospect, if I knew back then what I know now I would have put effort into gaining a knowledge of myself, the knowledge of God, the knowledge of time, and the knowledge of what must be done. The best knowledge that anyone

2

of you can have is to equip yourself to master the circumstances, that up to this point, have mastered us. That is the knowledge of self, the knowledge of God, the knowledge of the time, and the knowledge of what must be done. And when you have that kind of knowledge my young brothers and sisters, then you have the key to open the jail door. Further, you have the key not only to open the jail, but to master the circumstances that will or have brought you to jail; circumstance that you have no control over, circumstances that with knowledge you become the master of. Just like Nelson Mandela and Malcom X came out of prison and became masters of the circumstances that brought them to prison. Both of them, free men mentally, began to free people spiritually with the truth that they had found.

An so, I say that to end this short letter to you, all my young brothers and sisters, that after each dark night comes a brighter day. Sincerly, your brother, servant, and friend in making humanity great again.

Edward (Sababu) Cook
J-77594

Sebastian Loncaric

The Next Time

The next time, I will let God guide my way.
The next time, I will cherish the gift of life.
The next time, I will die

                rather than kill.

The next time, I will love.
The next time, I will die

                rather than kill.

The next time, I will love

                rather than hate.

The next time, I will give my life

                rather than take one.

The next time, I will love

                rather than hate.

The next time.

Sebastian Loncaric
BG-1138

A Letter to My Victims

Dear Hector,

   I've been putting this off for over 11 years. Its not that I haven't thought about you, you've touched my mind, my heart, and my soul.

   A lot has happened in that time. And I'm not exactly sure where to begin. This is a very difficult letter to write. I've taken so much from you and your family. By now you know everything, but I still feel that I owe you an explanation. Although nothing, nothing excuses my actions. No. There is no acceptable explanation. And this letter is not about me, it's an apology. I had no right. My issues do not justify my actions.

   I'm sorry Hector. I am truly sorry. There aren't words to describe how horrible I feel for what I did to you, to your family; for the unbearable pain I caused your parents, your siblings. I know they love you. I took your life. It wasn't mine to take. I had no right. I robbed you of your future. Who knows what the future would have held. You could have gone on to do great things, been with your family, had children, and God knows what else.

   This has really hit home lately. My youngest child, my 15 year old daughter just got released from the ICU at a childrens hospital. She has really bad seizures. I feel so helpless, there is nothing I can do for my baby.

   It made me think of your parents. I can't even imagine what they went through, go through, how helpless they felt. That sort of pain never goes away. The pain of losing a child. The pain of not being able to protect your baby. The desperate desire to take the affliction on to yourself. I hurt so bad, and my daughter is alive. How much worse it is for your parents.

   The pain I caused is unforgiveable. A woman named Jennifer Hubbard once wrote: "I have lived with numbing cold that courses through a mothers veins as she lays her baby to rest in frozen earth." I am so sorry.

   And what about you? Having to watch all of your loved ones suffer. I can't say

In Retrospect

Knowing then what I know now, how would I have done it different? I would change almost everything. So how do I begin? At the start I suppose. If I start there everthing that follows should fall in place.

I was born in Rijeka, Croatia. Yugoslavia, back in 1977. Croatia did not gain independence until the 90's. I lived there with my grandparents until 1981 or 82, I can't remember which. I got my "green card" in 1982, but I think I lived in New Jersey before that.

Shortly after I was born my mother left me with my grandparents and went to Germany. In the hopes of providing me with a better life. Not a lot of opportunity in Yugoslavia during the Cold War. Even though Tito kept us out of the control of the Soviet Union, Yugoslavia was not a part of the Warsaw Pact. The region has however been in turmoil since the beginning of time. I loved it. I love it. It's hom

1981 or 1982 my mother came back for me. I was 4 or 5. She had gotten married to an American G.I., who was stationed at an airforce base near Trier, Germany. my mom was a cocktail waitress at a club when they met. I hated him. He was big and ugly and American. He didn't speak my language. He was different than anything I had ever encountered before .

Knowing what I do now, I would have totally embraced my moms husband. My dad. The only one I've ever known. As far as I know, my biological father has been in prison my entire life. All I know of him is the stories my grandma told me.

My dad, the man my mom married when I was three, that's my dad. And I love him. He was a hard man. Not at all what I was used to. He hit me. No one else had. He did it only when I messed up, as a correction. He is a really big man. He was a bodyduilder; then a powerlifter; now a strength coach. I don't think he realized how hard he hit. How much it hurt. How much it hurt my pride. How uncomfortable I felt around him.

1

My point is, he did the best that he could. He loved. He loves me as his own.
I know that now. I wish I would have loved him. He did cool things with me when
I was kid. He took me to see WWF wrestling. He took me to see the Harlem Globe
Trotters, and all sorts of other things. He expressed interest and encouraged
me in sports. He was even one of my coaches when I played high school football.
I went to the gym with him form age 11 to age 18. He made sure that I had a
roof over my head, clothes on my back, food in my stomache, and all the rest of
my necessities. And then some. Because of him I saw the world. Even now, he is
the only one that consistently writes to me. I appreciated none of it. I re-
belled at every turn. I was an ingrate. I love him so much now, but I should've
loved him then.

My mom too. I was mad at her well into adulthood. For what? For taking me
away from Croatia, from grandparents, from everything I knew and loved. My mom
gave up everything she knew and loved to give me a better life. A life with
more opportunity, and I hated her for it.

She wrote to me a few years back. She apologized to me for not doing a better
job. She explained that I didn't come with an instruction manual, and that she
tried her best. I have children of my own now. I better understand how I made
her feel. How she felt watching me destroy my life. How she felt when I, her
only son, rejected her. Rejected her love.

I wish that I could go back. I would cherish her like every mother deserves
to be cherished. She was a cold woman when I was growing up. I know now that's
because of the culture she was raised in; post World War II Yugoslavia. My
grandmother was an alcoholic and abused my mom. Another thing I know now. My
poor mother. One of my biggest regrets. I try now, but how many years of an-
guish am I responsible for?

In retrospect, I would have lived my entire life different. I understand
what's important now. Life is important. Family is important. God is important.

2

If I would've understood, if I would've kept those four things in mind at all times. If I made all my decisions with those four values in mind... I would've never went wrong, and my life would've been completely different. And so would the lives of all those who I have adversely affected.

In retrospect, I would change so much. But if I start here, everything else would fall into place.

Sebastian Loncaric
BG-1138

Donel Poston

The Next Time

I have never felt any accomplishment or pleasure
from an endeavor that facilitated pain,
especially when the slain is an innocent man
oblivious to the fact that his life is about to end.
There is no way to pretend that my involvement didn't infringe
on a life long journey for my victim's kid.
This ain't what the system did, its what the streets created,
A sick fixation that caused affliction to my community
because of all of my stupidity and selfish activity.
In hindsight, I hope the next time I got my mind right,
because my impusive psychosis has cost me a life sentence.
Everyday of my life I ask God for repentance.
How can I make amends when a life has ended?
How can I relieve the pain that's never ending?
I guess once I fix myself I can start giving,
I mean giving right now, so them blessings come back 'round,
because next time It'll be less crime and more love.
Next time It'll be more life and no blood.
Next time......Next time
I pray to God there isn't a next time,
because whose to say it won't be my time next.

Donel Poston
AT-2512

A Letter to My Victims

I often ask myself, "how did you start a day full of life only to end it by taking one?" The death of my victim was a culmination of a disastrous lifestyle that left many victims in its wake. I take full accountability for those who suffered on behalf of my actions.

Oftentimes, when you create a victim it's because of a selfish intent; what I need, what I want. This blind ambition to succeed at all cost no matter what comes of it. This is what happens when you move impulsively; when you blame everybody for everything and don't take responsibility for nothing.

There is no repairing death. There is no panacea, replacement, or alternative for a life lost. How do you fulfill a damaged heart when you have permanently taken a father who use to fill it with joy? You can't. The suffering is perpetual, and I am the cause of it.

I am sorry. I am a sorry ass individual who had no regard for others. I am sorry because I allowed my lifestyle to supersede a human life; sorry because I let my kids down and my mama down. I am sorry God, I ask for you forgiveness and for your mercy for all my decrepit actions.

However, since sorry is moot and it has never fixed nothing, what should I do from this time forward? Well, I have been changing the way I think. Not only have I begun to change the way I think, I'm trying to instill this new way of thinking in those who have the potential of making more victims. It is my duty to help end the cycle of victimization. I may never be able to give back the life I took, but I can make a conscious effort to stop another one from being taken.

Sincerly, my deepest sentiments goes out to my victim's family. I will forever be in debt for the pain I have caused. Please forgive me, I am now making a vaild attempt at writing my wrongs.

Donel Poston
AT-2512

In Retrospect

I would like to begin by saying that I am very remorseful and sad that my victim had to die. Because of my disordered thinking and warped beliefs about life an innocent man named Lionel Fluker had to die. This project is dedicated to all the victims that I've created over the years. Please forgive me for my stupidity, ignorance, and selfishness. I truly apologize for all the pain I've caused and the victims made by me, big or small.

As a child, growing up in Oakland, CA, I was loved and nutured by two caring parents. My two older brothers loved me as well. I idolized my brothers, they were my role models.

However, the 80s introduced the crack epidemic. My brothers began smoking crack in Junior high school. Crack was a mainstay in my neighborhood, paraded around under the illusion that it was a rich amn's high. Alongside my brothers, my parents were caught in the convoluted catastrophe that ultimately caused chaos in my community. Oddly, I never missed a meal, clothes to wear, or having a roof over my head. My parents always loved me, regardless of anything, they gave me everything, but due to the times and the circumstances, this invasion was actively tearing my family a part.

My first introduction of drugs in my parents room. I think I may have stumbled upon a triple beem scale and that pique my interest. All this negative exposure shaped my being. Everyone in my neighborhood had someone affected by drugs. The corners and the housing authority apartments were saturated with young dudes peddling dope. I watched it destroy my happy home and create monsters out of my brothers, my parents, and my community. Crack consumed their existence.

I was able to excel in school, but at some point I realized that I wasn't getting any recognition or admonishment for the things that I was doing. I started drifting. Because my parents weren't interested in what I was doing, I took it upon myself to indulge in marijauna and alcohol, eventually I would run away.

1

The streets were vicious, I had a love hate relationship with it. I used my
wit and intelligence to do criminal activity. This began a life-long struggle
with stealing and defrauding people. I learned early about crimes that weren't
prevalent at the time amongst urban dwelling teenagers; credit card and check
fraud. I moved to selling drugs and robbery, all stemming from a addiction,
something I never anticipated.

Furthermore, as I aged, I became slicker, cocky, and stupid. Careless were
my actions. After multiple stints in prison, and a haze of drug induced
thoughts, I had became something that I said I would never become, an addict.
I manage to have a bevy of babies and a serious case of denial. I began to
make impulsive decisions that would continuously land me in prison a countless amount of times.

Through all the turmoil and irrational decisions, I found myself lying in
the hospital with a fatal gunshot wound that nearly ended my life. I took my
life for granted, because as soon as I was released from the hospital I was
back on the corner dealing drugs with no regard for my family and children.
This lead to an even bigger problem, carring a weapon. This lifestyle was
manifested from warped beliefs that I thought everybody possessed. I believed
that since I had been shot that I needed to defend myself, better yet, prove
myself. What an idiot.

Moreover, I found myself living a destructive lifestyle, for some reason it
felt like I needed to have a gun to make a point, "I ain't no punk." Some how
I found myself in a situation that was unmanageable. The weapon that I was
carrying caused pain to so many families, and now I'm paying for it.

In retrospect, I would've never jumped ship on school. I would've asked for
help, never running from my situation an abandoning my children and their
mothers. I was so smart but so ever ignorant and dumb. I wanted to live my life
on center stage, but clearly my ego shattered my dreams at succeeding on any

stage. As I look back, I am frighten at what I had become. I never realized my full potential and what I could accomplish in life. I wanted more for myself then, but not like I want more for myself now.

On the other hand, if I had known then what I know now, I would've invested in my future. Maybe I could've been the reason why my parents stop using drugs. I could have used my situation as a catalyst for other situations. I wish I would have been a strong closer instead of a careless beginner. What if I could have used all my knowledge and insight to help my community stick together and prevent senseless acts of violence form occuring.

God willing, I intend to live my life finding my true purpose, giving unrelentlessly. I hope now that I have begin to live my life selfless that I can continue to repay society for all the harm that I've caused. I am ashamed, and I apologize for being a bad father to my lovely daughters, a tyrant to my baby mothers, and defiant to my mother who has always been there for me. Please forgive me for the pain I've caused to the Fluker family and all the people I've tormented over my destructive life. Sincerly, a man trying to come to grips for what I've done.

Donel Poston
AT-2512

Drew Allee

The Next Time

This is a poem about who I once was and all that I've done,
Because during a robbery, I killed an innocent man with a gun.
This poem is also about the many victims I've made, and lives torn apart,
Words can never explain the sorrows of my heart.
I'm ashamed and sickened by all the pain I've caused,
had I only stopped a second to pause...
I was too busy being a self-centered, inconsiderate, shell of a human being,
these are ways of a real "dope fiend."
My callous and careless decisions, guided by my desires of the moment,
are the root of this tragic disaster, I'll forever own it.
I've caused more damage than I can ever repair,
I'm sorry to everyone I've caused pain and despair.
I'd also like to take this opportunity,
to extend my deepest condolences to the community.
I'm a completely changed man now and I've shown it,
I spend the rest of my days living atonement.
The next time I ever find myself suffering in silence,
I promise to reach out for help and guidance.
For the rotten fruit my role in your lives continues to bare,
you're all forever in my thoughts and prayers.
I'm sorry from the bottom of my heart.
Very respectfully.

Drew Allee
BA-8058

A Letter to My Victims

I am writing this letter to reach out to the many victims throughout the many communities that I've brought great harm to.

I am hoping this letter will bring some type of healing. Words will never completely be able to express how truly sorry I am for murdering an innocent man and scaring countless others during my robberies. I've reached a deeper understanding of the avalanche of atrocity I've sent crashing down onto entire communities, of the multitude of victims I've created, that are forever impacted by the actions of one coward with a gun.

I bare total responsibility for the life I've taken. By using a gun, I devalued every single life who stood in my way. I was a careless, inconsiderate, coward, and am fully responsible for my actions. Since my incarceration I've done alot of self-reflection, therapy, and have taken my personal inventory. I now see as to how and why I've come to commit such horrendous crimes.

There is no excuse for my actions. I'm so very sorry to every single individual person I've affected during the course of my crimes, and to every person I've ever hurt in any way throughout the course of my entire life. I'm sorry from the bottom of my heart. I will live the rest of my life in amends. In an effort to help more people than I've hurt. I'm no longer the shell of a person I was before my incarceration and I'll never be that thing again. I'll forever be a builder, never again a destroyer. Never will I hurt another person as long as I live.

I extend my deepest heartfelt sorrows and regrets to each and every victim I've ever made.

Drew Allee
BA-8058

In Retrospect

Let me start by saying that there is no excuse for the crimes I've committed, and without a doubt, I deserve to be here in prison, for life, for the things I've done. This is my brief story as to how and why I'm here in prison writing this.

From an early age I was on my own, my dad was there, but that's about all he was, just there; he was not very supportive as a parent should be. I used to get beat up when I was a child, as far back as I can remember, my younger brother and I would constantly get beat up by our dad; kicked, punched, slapped, spit on, called every foul name you can think of, and had anything within my dad's reach thrown at us.

My mom left and moved out of state, as early as I can remember, she was gone. We grew up on welfare, very poor. I used to get picked on and bullied at school alot for being poor and different. My dad was a drug addict and alcoholic every since I can remember. He always had a 40 ounce King Cobra malt liquor in his hand and had to be buzzed up, no matter what we did. I didn't know my dad was a drug addict until I was older and became one myself.

At the age of 19 or 20 years old I started using methamphetamine, a "friend" turned me onto it during a tough time in my life, addiction ran in my family and was in my blood. I started out using occasionally, and soon the addiction set in and I started using daily. Then, the love of my life came into the picture.

I got her pregnant, and we had our son. I quit using meth cold turkey when she got pregnant While she was pregnant we got married. So here I am on the road to having all I ever wanted in this life. A happy family, which I never had growing up. I had such a wonderful vision of my future as a husband, and now father.

Not long after our marriage, and birth of our son, I started running into

1

relationship problems and life problems. I didn't know how to fix or deal with these issues on my own, nor did I know how to get help. So inevitably, our marriage fell apart. Not even two years after our marriage and committment of "till death do us part", it was over. She took our son and moved out.

The very next day after my wife and son left, I picked right back up where I left off, using meth and partying all my pain away. I considered myself a "functioning" drug addict. And justified my using; thinking "well I don't have a family anymore, I work, I have all my own stuff, I'm a grown man and now I can do what I want."

I've never felt more pain inside then the day my wife and son left. I felt all my visions of having a family stripped away, gone, and never to return. At this point in my life this was the most traumatic event I've ever experienced.

The only way I knew how to cope was using drugs: meth, weed, alcohol, anything that would numb the pain; getting high one way or another, all day every day, just numbing the pain.. At work, home, in public, anywhere, anytime. This went on for years, never getting over the pain of my family falling apart. I had multiple failed relationships, could no longer hold a job, my emotions and mental health were spiraling out of control. Because of being on my own at a young age and having to figure things out on my own, I figured I was the only one who knew best how to help myself. And if I couldn't help myself, then nobody could help me.

I tried quitting drugs many times. Every time I quit I didn't want to live anymore. I had become so dependent on these drugs and being high all the time, that when I wasn't high, life just felt dull, the only thing that I enjoyed was being high. If I wasn't high then all the pain I'd been surpressing would re-surface, and that pain was unbearable. I honestly felt like if I didn't stay high i was going to kill myself, because I hated my life, who I was, and what I'd become.

2

I gave up on life, I gave up on my son and family. I gave up caring about anything anymore.

Every way I tried to quit doing drugs failed, no matter what I did I kept going back to getting high. So in my warped mind I had decided that the only way I could quit drugs was to get locked up and then I'd be forced to deal with my problems and I wouldn't be able to run any longer.

I had the bright idea to start robbing stores with fake toy guns, to lash out at society, to support my drug habit, and when I got caught I could finally go to prison and get cleaned up. I had robbed several stores by now with fake guns.

now I've been awake, high on meth without sleep for about three weeks. I came into possession of a real pistol now, I'd became more brazen. During the final robbery, it went bad, and I shot and killed the clerk. I was arrested the very next morning for multiple armed robberies and an attempted murder. I was charged, convicted, and guilty of first degree murder and sentenced to life without the possibilty of parole.

I am in prison now and have been alcohol and drug free since my arrest in 2015. This isn't exactly how I planned on coming to prison. In retrospect, I couldn't have been more wreckless. I have killed an innocent man, devastated families, bystanders, and entire communities. I have left countless victims in my wake.

Since my incarceration I've sought help for my mental health, I've taken much therapy, many self-help groups, and have forced myself to take a deep look into my inner self to see exactly why and how I came to commit the horrible acts that brought me to this point.

If only I knew then what I know now how to reach out for help when I run into a problem that I don't know how to fix on my own; how to vent my frustrations in healthy ways And no matter how things seem it's never the end of the world. I should have never touched drugs and alcohol, and I should have got help when I needed it.

3

Had I known then what I know now, I would have never resorted to criminal behaviors and actions as a way to lash out or as a means to seek help. These are the thoughts and actions of a disturbed and distorted individual, and a coward, to afraid to deal with his problems.

I am now properly equipped to cope with lifes stressors in healthy ways that don't include violence or mind altering substances. I'll never again use violence. I'll never hurt another person as long as I live.

I'll continue to learn everything I can to change lives, no matter where I am, for the better. In hopes of preventing others from taking the path I chose. I'll spend my entire life making amends to those I've hurt and giving back anyway I can.

I hate who I was and what I've done. I'm no longer that shell of a person. No one deserves to go through what I put my victims through. I'm so very sorry... No more victims. Respectfully,

Drew Allee
BA-8058

4

The Next Time

The next time, the next time, why not before,
my humanity was filed away, locked behind a door.
How could I cause this tremendous amount of pain,
cruelness upon another in this world has no gain.
Guilt haunts the foundation of my soul,
my destructive actions have caused a heavy toll.
Shame upon me too much too bare,
I am responsible for many peoples despair.
Sorrow echoes the depths of my heart,
A resounding feeling that tears me apart.
Callousness which I have shown other people,
consumes my conscious it has no equal.
Cowardly is what my actions have portrayed,
A generational magnitude of survivors I've made.

The next time, the next time, moving forward these days,
life has infinite value in a multitude of ways.
The next time my life will be centered around amends,
I seek to help others through my new hearts lens.
The next time I will make better decisions,
for compassion has grown to be my new vision.
The next time I will put myself in anothers shoes,
my debt to victims is something I'll never lose.
The next time my coping skills firmly in place,
healthy processing of lifes hardships transformed into grace.
The next time honesty will connect my emotion,
truth will reveal my non-violent devotion.
The next time my kindness will shine strong and bright,
in hopes of healing my wrongs and setting things right.

Anonymous

A Letter to My Victims

I am so sorry for murdering you, for how after years of kindness and friendship towards me, I betrayed your trust and that kindness with the most extremely
heinous act of murder. Today I see how I used our friendship, the feeling of
safety you had in my presence, and the lack of suspicion you would have going
some place with me. How over the years we spoke about many things that were
important to us, shared multiple adventures together, built a friendship, how
then for my own selfishness, cruel and cowardly emotions, rather than tell you
how I was feeling, or, what was going on, I murdered you from behind while you
were defenseless.

I took your future away from you, your right to live a long life that was to
include you continuing to grow into becoming a man, a son, a brother, and a
future father. I took away you seeing your sister graduate high school. Instead,
she received a scholarship in your honor. Seeing your sister become a teacher,
get married, and have children; I took that away from you. Also, I found out
that your father became ill and that your mother suffered deep depression. I
robbed all of you of the chance to be a family and support each other during
these life events.

I am sorry for many things: how I left your body out in that field, how I
spoke lies about what I did to you in an attempt to avoid taking responsibility
for my horrendous actions, how I deceived your family and friends by telling
them I had no idea what happened to you, how I justified the reason for murdering you due to my misguided loyalty. There is no excuse for my callous behavior
and I know I caused unending sorrow for your family and friends. I knew the
difference between right and wrong and I am solely responsible and guilty for
murdering you. I am so very sorry.

I understand how my lifestyle and choices were my own. I caused a tidal wave
of destruction and created countless victims throughout my life. I devastated

1

a community and brought fear and grief into existence through my careless and violent actions.

I want you to know I often think about my actions, so that I can be sure I will never behave in that way again. I have learned through self-help groups, therapy, and intensive introspection to correct my negative thoughts and behaviors. I am determined today to walk a life of service in order to make a positive difference and never create another victim or cause another person to become a survivor. Today I focus on avenues for helping other people network and increase positive relationships and opportunities centered around the daily use of social and coping skills in healthy ways and manners.

Anonymous

In Retrospect

If I knew then what I know now I would of never created a victim in my life.
I would of never embraced criminal thinking and committed the destructive and
violent acts that created a multitude of victims and caused future generations
to become survivors. there are no justifications for the crimes I have committed. I am responsible for all of them as I sit here writing this 21 years into
a life sentence guilty and convicted of murder.

I was born to older parents who had been married for 15 years prior to me
coming along. I was an only child. We lived in a small town all under the same
roof. My childhood home was emotionally distant. My parents worked full time
and I was raised in the homes of day care providers and at school. In my
earliest memories I remember feeligs loved and cared for and tucked into bed
with a hand on my chest. However, I remember this ending when very young too.
I was hurt by this and felt confused as to why this stopped. Feelings of abandonment and loneliness started early for me. In my household I was provided
with all the tangible things I needed: food, clothing, hygiene, shelter, and
schooling. The intangible things were absent; communication was rare and I
cannot remember my dad ever saying he loved me.

The first time I felt soul crushing confusion and shame is when my father
walked in on me being molested, through coercion, by an older friend at the
age of 10 years old. He didn't say anything, but I vividly recall how I felt;
first confused, then overwhelmed by shame and embarrassment. I now realize
that what I thought were acts of caring and friendship were wrong. I felt em-
barrassed, hurt and betrayed, then angry. Moving forward, deeper negative feelings of these emotions surfaced when my father never checked on me or seemed to
care how I felt about it, even though it ended that day. I felt shame and embarrassment that he knew of this unmentionable event whenever I was around him.
This created a feeling that I did not matter to him and I felt confusion and hurt.

1

I suffered with insecurities, inadequacies, trust issues (with peers too) and low self-esteem for years. I found that my feelings of anger and betrayal developed into resentment, hate, and rage (which I mostly repressed). I learned to have secrets and never talk about what I was feeling. I never spoke about this until 25 years later. I accepted, as I was taught by my father, that it was up to me to figure things out and deal with it on my own.

After the molestation I felt lost and distraught with low self-worth. I went and committed my first criminal acts: vandalism and petty theft. I felt power and control as my hurtful emotions and low self-worth receded. I didn't get caught and the rewards I received from these negative behaviors taught me that consequences were not a major deterrent, since the rewards to me were worth the feeling. This started the process of emotional and mental disassociation and apathy regarding the feelings and rights of others or any need for me to take responsibility for my choices and actions.

When I was introduced to alcohol and marijuana I found that the intoxication would numb my feelings of inadequacy and negative emotions for awhile. Along with this reward, I realized my older peers seemed to like me more and accept me more for using. I began to prove myself to them by my willingness to engage in substance abuse and criminal behavior. I saw them as my family. My distorted views entitled me to do whatever I wanted, so I did just that. I only felt selfishly sorry for myself when I would get caught, and only   long enough to get myself out of trouble.

I developed a need to be "that guy" and was willing to "be down" doing anything to prove it. I had already given myself the right to ignore the laws of society thereby devaluing both property and people. I utilized this stance to protect my distorted behavior and further separate myself from rational thinking and responsibility. Among my peers I rationalized that if certain "fabricated" situations ever happened that I would "take a (fictional) person out (kill)"

2

if a violation of these "thought up" situations took place. I never truly felt
I would ever actually murder anybody. I now understand that subconsciously or
not I had given myself permission to murder another human being.

At the age of 16 years old my ingrained negative and criminal behaviors found
me faced with a "thought up" situation where murder was brought up and I followed
through with it. I quickly realized what I had done and was overwhelmed with the
terror of this horrible act. Faced with this terror and the responsibility of
what I had done, I fell back on my past criminality and never-ending attempts to
avoid taking responsibilty. Rather than contact the authorities my only thoughts
were to get as far away from what I had done and to cover up my involvement. I
was caught and convicted.

Coming into prison I found myself back in the same emotional state I experienced growing up; fear, insecurities, inadequacies, trust issues, and low self-
esteem. For many years I continued my criminality and destructive and violent
actions by justifying my need for safety and acceptance in this violent environ-
ment.

It took many years into my incarceration for me to realize the true impact of
my crimes upon my community. Sadly, after a pile up of my own personal hardships
in life, I finally snapped out of my selfish and distorted thinking and behaviors.
Laid bare, at the age 25 years old, I started the process of growing up. I no
longer wanted to feel numb to the reality of my life or how my actions have
affected other people and ripped out the heart of my community. The heart was the
person I murdered. And I am the cancer that I poisoned everything it touched.

Around that time someone asked me how I had gotten to this point in my life.
I was speechless for a time reflecting on thoughts and feelings that I have
never wanted to let in. I became aware of the numerous heartaches I have created
for so many of my victims throughout my life prior to my incarceration and during
it. I began to take full responsibility for all my choices, both good and bad,

3

and find that I have many regrets and a very deep sorrow. I am filled with immense shame and sadness for each person I have hurt and the ripple effect of pain and suffering I have caused which continues to devastate everything it touches to this day.

Today, I have been alcohol and drug free for 17 years. I am a member of a positive non-violence community. I share my thoughts and feelings freely today. I am equipped with coping skills and a newfound understanding that I must always make positive choices even in unfortunate circumstances. Today I share the skills I learn in hopes of helping other people work through their problems. I have a wide support system in place to lean on whenever I need advice or just an ear willing to listen. Today I help my community to ensure the ripple effects I produce are positive and healthy.

I will continue to be in a state of constant rehabilitation for the rest of my life. I will be responsible to my community by volunteering my time to improve it and every person who relys upon it. My responsibility to humanity is to live with the negative things I have done while always being aware of how these actions, and my future actions, will affect the world around me.

If I knew then what I know now...I would reach out for help whenever faced with overwhelming events, thoughts, or feelings...have the confidence to say something isn't right and correct it...never use alcohol or drugs to escape life... always respect the rights and property of other people...never commit violence upon another human being.

Anonymous

The Next Time

It took awhile to see the significance
to feel the impact of what happened
Not from my point-of-view, but from yours.
To look into the sky and see your eyes bring the rain...
Or even into mine
feeling the deepest and most profound sense of shame.
For years I always wondered
Why God told Cain,
that he heard the voice of his brother's blood cry out
on the day that he was slain.
But, I think I get it
and I finally understand.
It's only when you truly love life
and every single thing created by God's hand
that you can't help but hear the distant screams
of evil men's deeds
ring in your ears over, and over, and over again.
Brother, you died for nothing.
And I bear the guilt becuase I could've said something
but I just went along.
So the price of my life in comparison is cheap, knowing
it's your innocent blood that weeps
from the still fresh dripping wet stains on my palms.
So often I think of your moms,
and I can't begin to imagine her hurt.
Because what I so willingly gave away
is incomparable to what was taken from her.
I rewind to the last day we talked,
wishing I just could've listened.
You spoke to me words almost prophetic in their wisdom.
You warned me of the company I kept
gave me perspective on my loyalties.
It's only now that I'm a man
that I can see what you were showing me.
Today, I find peace only when I release what once was
a mere shadow of a thought that I'd keep behind latchkey.

James Wilson

The Next Time

Why should there ever be a sequence of
events that end in such a horrible tragedy?

Next time is not an option!

Why should there be countless lives lossed,
innocent people hurt, what's the tax payers
cost? Communities destroyed, families
broken apart.

Next time is not an option!

Now it's time to live and let live. That's
what time it is!

James Wilson
AU-5200

A Letter to My Victims

What was done in the dark came to the light, giving me an opportunity to clearly see and confront my misdeeds. Not suprisingly, I stand before you and the world guilty and convicted for horrible crimes; not only in court, but in my heart.

I come before you repentant, with legal formalities now set aside, unveiling another one of my hiding places, I write this letter fully contrite, exposed and begging for your unearned forgiveness. I make this plea to any human being that I've injured, in any way, throughout my entire life. I am sincerly and forever sorry for my actions.

I am a 44 year old man. I have no chidren. I cannot begin to fathom the depth of pain experienced when one is taken or injured unjustifiably. Who can weigh a parents grief? I cannot imagine.

My willingness to accept guilt and the consequences for my actions only tell the beginning of the story, not the ending. I have so much work to do to prove myself and improve my life; certainly, it will be a life-time journey an uphill battle. But, going forward I will seek help from qualified people, further my education, and work to stay in the light more than anything! And if possible "save" some lives. I accept all my challenges. And I am under no illusion that I could right the wrong of taking a human life. But, I pray that God has given you the strength to face your own loss and challenges.

Once again, please find it in your heart to forgive me. I am sorry.

James Wilson
AU-5200

In Retrospect

I have spent half of my life incarcerated. I am 44 years old. 20 plus years is a long time for a man to spend away from home.

But, I am grateful to have had a place that was once called "home"; even the dysfunctional family that occupied it was far better than having no family at all. We learned to "function". My mother was 14 years old when she had her first child. She managed to have 7 of us and survive with her scruples in tact. I have never met a stronger woman. In the late 70s public assistance housing for a single parent (low income families) came to the "rescue" and all 8 of us piled into a four bedroom apartment in this place we called "The Projects".

Pasadena, California, has a reluctant ghetto. Most of the poverty, gangs and crime exist in the north-west part of the city and most of the surrounding area is middle class and obviously affluent. It was the perfect place for poor black kids to play the wishful thinking game we naively called "that's my house" or "that's my car" as we drove past all the luxury items that encircled us.

We were a poor family but I wouldn't say we were broke. Moms always found a way to make, as she'd put it, ends meet.

It would be better to say that I've went to sleep many times half full than to claim I went to bed on an empty stomache. thinking back, it was bad but there were people worst off. When the newly created gang phenomenon of the 70s met the crack epidemic in the 80s the only stable force was my mother, Connie. All 7 of her siblings (my maternal grandmother had 7 children as well) found themselves at the wrong end of the crackpipe followed by two of my brothers pushing the lethal substance. It was at this junction that the legacy of drugs, gangs, and incarceration took root in my familys story, turning possibilities into horror stories. I caught my first drug charge at 13, less than 6 months after entering Junior High School. I escaped the courts with probation but being attracted to the local gang and sustaining my drug selling brought me

1

direct condemnation from my mother without any reprieve; she kicked me out at 14 years old insisting that no longer was drug dealers, like my two brothers, tolerated in her home.

My father came around but he had another residence and side chick. After increasing heart disease he lost his strength and along with it the fear he onced pumped into our hearts by way of his brutal "extension chord" whoopings. Not to mention my gang mentality told me that no man, including him, was permitted to get away with putting their hands on me anymore. The moral voice of my mother and fathers stern hand were simultaneously broken after gangs and drugs entered the picture. The next scene was the streets, and not too long afterwards, many stints in juvenile camps and California Youth Authority. I was 21 years old by the time I looked up and maxed out from "Y.A". Not willing to look up for long, I was back in custody, now an adult game, facing charges for homicide and assault with a deadly weapon. I pled out for 14 years (7 + 7 ran concurrent) and made my way off to prison as the next phase in what seemed like the intended life-style for poor black males in north-west Pasadena. I am currently in prison on a second murder "plead". This time the stakes were higher: the District Attorneys office filed a capital case on me, a case that would keep me in L.A. County Jail almost 10 years "fighting for my life" and my family.

It was in L.A. County Jail in a single cell (High Power Module) that I began to take stock of my life and all the destruction I had wrought on other human beings and my community. I had been a monster.

Higher power is intended to operate like a makeshift "special Housing Unit" (S.H.U). In this form of isolation, with the so-called worst of the worst, you either come out improved or morally and mentally impoverished. I chose the former. Only death could take me lower than I was. But, I not only wanted to live; actually, I wanted to become better, even if my final resting place was

2

gonna be death row. I knew I could have a life no matter what the outcome of my case was. I couldn't change the past but I could improve my future. I discovered meditation and world history through Nagy, a former buddhist chaplain in the county jail. We became great friends and he walked with me through my catharsis for over 8 years and introduced me to my "spiritual" big brother and sister Rabbi Brian and Jane Mayer. The work Nagy had begun in me they took over the "New Project" of taken the ghetto (conditioned failure) out of me. As a Muslim I was learning first hand that God could work through anyone to help me — A buddhist (Nagy), A Jew (Brian), or a Christian (Jane). Love, in all its forms of expression, reached into my darkned cell and heart and begun a process of lifting me up. I started to see the words and love of my biological mother taken on new meaning in my mind through my new spiritual family.

One excuse I did not have was the absentee mother or the standard claim that no one cared. My oldest brother, who never chose the streets (who got married, went to college, and worked) fought hard against my other brothers negative example and the street life to pull me toward the light (right). A few teachers and deans at schools I attended tried desperately to steer me on the right course. My mothers standard refrain was: "I did not raise you to be like this". She did not use drugs or sleep around with strange men. Neither did she run the streets or have "friends" hanging around her house with her kids. Moms worked and took care of her children. No, she wasn't perfect; there were flaws. But, had I listened to her jail and gangs would not have been part of my destiny.

Looking back, in retrospect, I can see the model she intended for all of her kids in my little brother who never joined; A gang, wasn't violent and never went to prison. But, this moral knowledge had to take root in me, grow, withstand various trials, and mature. Now, at 44 years old, I am really living my best life, even while in prison. I am no longer in a gang. I am drug and alcohol

3

free. I try to live a non-violent life. I have developed into a role model for other men in the prison community, and I mentor others about living a positive and productive life.

Finally, I got it! Now, I am paying it forward. Crime, violence, and prison no longer define me. I am free inside.

James Wilson
AU-5200

Brian Fiore

The Next Time

A young mind, impressionable, seeking acceptance, and attention
sobriety taken for granted, allured and infatuated with a secret life.
What are drugs? They seem so wonderful, are they the answer to my prayers?
The next time I'll know and find out finally.
Wow! It worked. I feel great, and look at all my new friends,
I feel so cool and I'm finally accepted.
Who would ever want to keep this gift a secret?
I think the next time I'll try something stronger;
If I feel this good now I can't wait for the next time.
What happened? I don't feel so good anymore;
this will be the last time. I'll quit the next time.
Why can't I quit. The next time will be my last;
It's alright because I know I'm in control,
the next time will be my last.
They said I did what!? I wouldn't ever do that!
How did I end up in prison? What happened to all my friends?
When will the next time come for me to walk outside these fences?
I finally understand, the next chance I get I'll pull these poisonous hooks out of me,
the next time I'll be strong enough to say NO,
The next time I'll surround myself with friends dedicated to sobriety,
the next time I'll seek help from my higher power rather than substances to get
me higher. The next time I won't be lulled by false feelings,
the next time I'll make amends for my wrongs,
the next time I'll live a life worth living.

Brian Fiore

A Letter to My Victims

Dear David,

I am truly sorry. There is nothing I can say or do to bring you back and I wish it were different. My actions took you away from all that you loved and enjoyed. I severed any chance of you reaching your hopes, dreams, and goals. You were twenty-one years old with a life ahead of you and my actions cut that short.

I wish I had not been such a coward because I know both of our lives would have been different. You had a wonderful job opportunity lined up where your constructional skills would have designated you a foreman on the site. You were even generous enough to think of me and offer me a position. It was my misguided choices and greed that prevented this and ultimately led you to your death. By my actions leading to your death I created numerous vicitms, with you being the primary one.

No longer will you be able to enjoy life's preciousness and struggles. I took you away from your son who must now go through life without a father. You wont be able to give him the much needed guidance a young boy needs to help him grow into a man. You won't be there for his first day of school, his first girlfriend, his first heartbreak, his first fight, teaching him how to drive a car, blessing his marriage, or even experiencing grandchildren.

I took you away from being able to help Holly raise your son and now she must struggle as a single parent. I took you away from your fiancé, Kyrie, whom you were getting ready to marry and start a new life with. I took you away from your mom, aunt, and brother. I can only imagine the pain and suffering I have caused them to endure with your absence and death. To cause added pain I did this on Mother's Day. On a day that is supposed to be dedicated to women and mothers I have attached it to loss, pain, and sadness. I know these feelings can impact a person physically and can only imagine the anxiety, loss

1

of sleep. and poor health I have caused your love ones.

I took everything from you. My selfishness left a ripple filled with poison. You'll never get to laugh again, smile, love, shed tears, experience life's joys of birthdays, Christmas's, Thanksgiving, New Years, marriage, new children and the little things in life I took for granted but affect life so greatly. Words and actions can do nothing because your life gone is permanent. There is so much more to say to you David on how I destroyed your life and those who knew you and did not know you.

I am trying to do everything I can to understand the impact of my choices and be a better person than I was back then. I know there is no consolation to you or your loved ones. I am sorry David. I cannot bring you back or changed what happened but I am working at never creating another victim and I am trying to help others so they do not make the same poor choices I did. I never want another person to experience what I put you all through.

Brian Fiore

In Retrospect

My name is Brian Fiore and I was sentenced to over sixty-eight years in prison with multiple life sentences. Based upon the length of time one could speculate I was a career criminal, came from a family of low economic standing, or any other multitude of assumptions. Although some would be true, my life history and lifestyle would ultimately lead me behind bars.

I come from a middle class family. Be that as it may both of my parents were addicted to drugs. Fortunately my father was able to overcome his addiction but my mother could not. The last time I saw my biological mom I was five years old and my parents were arguing in the car. My mom opened up the door and literally walked out of my life. This experience would harm me in ways I did not understand and would not honestly deal with until I had already come to prison. I was confused, I didn't understand, and I felt abandoned and unloved.

Thankfully my dad would marry when I was seven to the woman I would call mom, and still call mom to this day. I would again feel these feelings when my parents divorced. To make matters worse my dad started dating my mom's best friend. I felt betrayed by my dad and resented him for his decision. There was physical and verbal abuse in my household. I have an older brother by three years who experienced the brunt of it all, but the abuses I went through led me to fear and resent my dad and would later turn to anger and hate. I used these feelings as a crutch and justification to use drugs and commit criminal acts as I grew into my early teenage years. I didn't understand how all my mixed emotions corrupted my mind. Rather than reaching out for help I chose to run from them and bury them with various substances.

Even at a young age I showed a lot of talent for baseball. When I was on the baseball field I felt free and was able to forget any of my problems. Since I was so good I would play with the older kids. I wanted their acknowledgement and acceptance and when I received it it boosted my self-confidence. I never quite

1

felt like I had an identity when I was growing up which left me impressionable.

In my household I noticed my dad talked to my brother about how we grew up and the things he did as a teenager. Around this time I was about thirteen years old. This was the same age I tried marijauna for the first time. For so long I had felt like something was missing from my life. I didn't realize it came from a fear of acknowledging my issues of abandonment with my mom and my anger towards my dad for his authoritarian style of parenting.

All of these issues led to a perfect storm that would throw me off course even futher. I thought my dad was hiding something from me when he would talk to my brother about what he did as a kid. In my immature mind I told myself I would find out for myself if he did not want to tell me. When I was using drugs I felt like nothing was wrong anymore. I felt like what was missing from my life was satisified through drugs. I allowed myself to find an identity in the criminal element. I was attracted to the rap music, the gangster movies, and violent video games. I thought this is who I wanted to be and because I wanted acceptance I was willing to do whatever it took to gain it.

I spent a lot of my youth running from the truth. I considered myself a man at the age of seventeen but I could not have been futher from the truth. I was lost and scared but covered all these feelings up with drugs and a fake life-style. When I was high I was able to live in denial and bolster my own self-image. I knew I was not who I was attempting to be so I overcompensated. No one ever challenged me about this so I was able to continue on with my family. Never giving my body a chance to sober up, my fantasy became my reality.

Even though I still loved baseball it would be some years later I would see how I took it for granted. Not just my sports career, but my educational career too. My friends, family, and coaches would encourage me to take care of myself and train but I did not care. The meaning was lost to my naivete and drug muddled brain. In my mind I was fine; I believed I was unstoppable and if I suffered any injuries I would take some pills and continue playing. With my education it was not as if I struggled because there were semesters of grade point averages of over 3.3. I would do well in the beginning semester so I could slack off in the second semester so my GPA would balance out. I would ditch school in order to get high and would attend my baseball games high. I see the folly in my choices. Had I been the man I proclaimed myself to be I would have been doing my best to prepare for a future.

Despite my efforts to sabotage myself I still graduated on time albeit at a different high school due to getting into a fist fight with my dad. I never once took accountability for my actions nor the consequences. I used multiple denial patterns — blame, minimize, rationalize, and avoidance to name a few. I had no clue what I was doing to myself — physically, mentally, and spiritually.

I had a chance to correct my life course attending some college classes. At this point in my life all I wanted was a job and the college classes I was taking to propel me forward in a career in water distribution or water treatment. I passed the classes and earned my state license for water distribution but I was lacking in effort to apply for a job. Not only was I lacking in effort, but I had contacts to help to get me a job. A fork in the road was presented to me and I chose wrongly. I had glamorized a criminal lifestyle for so long I intentionally sabotaged myself when it came to living an honest life. Even though it was lack of effort to obtain employment I told myself I had given it a genuine chance.

It was a culmination of my life choices that led to what happened next. Rather than taking ownership of my life and pursue my dreams I chose to live in my fantasy. I was not prepared for what a criminal life included. Not long after I would come to find out there was nothing glamorous about that lifestyle, there was no pause or stop button, and there was definitely no way to restart. I unleashed devastation that created a ripple effect that is still continuing on. I

3

shattered a family with loss of a son, father, brother, and husband; I created victims of a robbery who were impacted emotionally, finacially, physically, and spiritually; I put multiple police agencies through a night and lifetime of terror which extended into the four areas of victim impact; I wasted tens of thousands of dollars of hardworking taxpayers' money; I affected a peaceful community; and I am an embarassment to my family because I was not raised to be any of this.

I am responsible for all of this and an untold amount more. I am blessed to be alive and I now live with a purpose. Sobriety has given me the gift of clarity and I am living a life I hope will someday allow me to help others. It is my greatest hope to never create another victim, to help a youth overcome his or her burdens so as not to make the same poor choices I have made, and to make amends to all I have impacted. I have been able to shake my mask off and have found my identity in helping others, rather than continuing to negatively impact society — inside and outside of prison.

Brian Fiore

Program Outline

Write Our Wrongs Introduction

This writing project is a prisoner's initiative whose primary purpose is to demonstrate rehabilitation through remorse and restitution for victims of crime.

Write Our Wrongs borrows much of its title from the book, "Writing my Wrongs", by Shaka Senghor, a former prisoner, who changed his life while incarcerated and now spends his time speaking on victims impact related issues and also criminal justice reforms. Throughout this four month course each participant is required to commit to the following:

1. Writing a <u>poem</u> with a theme of remorse to victims,
2. Writing a <u>letter</u> to victims of ones crime and,
3. Writing a <u>short story (or lesson)</u> about the impact of crime on the lives of individuals and communities.

Moreover, the combined work will then be compiled and proposed for publishing. All proceeds from the book will go towards victims restitution and charity funds to assist children and poor families. **No participant will benefit financially from this project.**

Participation Requirement

Each participant must have the ability and be willing to do, in short, the following:

1. Qualified writing abilities. This is not an academic course, so our aim is not "teaching" others to write but, drawing upon those who've honed the skill already.
2. Demonstrable rehabilitative behavior. This course targets those inmates who are making strides to change their lives and renounce criminal activity and violent conduct.
3. Provide your own stationary and allocate personal time for each writing project.
4. Be willing to participate in victims impact group discussions throughout this course. (There is no requirement to speak about particular charges or names of victims, unless one volunteers this information).

Although this is a "writers project", we would be remissed in our duties if we didn't allocate time to discuss issues related to victims impact. So, some courses are designated specifically for this most important study and discussion.

5. Read copywright and publishing material provided to meet requirements for this goal during ones own time and in group setting to understand the publishing process.

6. Provide a single book of stamps (20 stamps) by the 5th week of the course. The stamps are to be used to pay for copyright expenses.

7. As initial admittance, provide the poem one desires to be part of his final work (letter, short story, etc.). The poem is an "initiative and entry fee."

8. Be willing to meet at least once a week for reviews, evaluations, and discussions per availability of sponsor or time allocation.

9. A victims pledge will be recited prior to every weekly meeting.

Further Insight

1. Each participants poem will be titled: **The Next Time.** The words for the poem are to be drawn from each persons own heart.

2. The title of each short story will be: **In Retrospect.** (The essential message is: "If I knew then what I know now.")

3. Finally, the victims impact letter will be titled: **A letter to my victims** and governed by the following principles:

   A. Remorse

   B. Accountability

   C. Responsibility and

   D. Amends

Each inmate participant will have a section (or chapter) which includes their written work-product bearing their names and CDCR numbers. **No Nicknames allowed.** Additional insight for this writing project will be provided during weekly meeting sessions (courses designated as "project overviews.")

We would like to thank everyone in advance for their participation in this project to giveback to individuals and communities that have suffered from our actions.

We can try to make things right by our efforts to write our wrongs.

                                                -Core Group Members

Write Our Wrongs writing, review and discussion sessions

Project Overview
Week 1

1. Pledge recited.
2. Participant introduction.
3. Initial Poem Submittal.
4. Copyright information passed out and read in group (Form TX, etc.)

Project Overview
Week 2

1. Pledge Recited.
2. Review and recital of poems by authors in group setting.
3. Discuss details of next writing project (victims impact letter).
4. Set time-table for final submission of letter.
5. Discuss actual book format and singnificance of entrys and their respective order.

Project Overview
Week 3

1. Pledge recited.
2. Victims impact study session.
3. Group discussion about letter to victims and their significance.

Project Overview
Week 4

1. Pledge recited.
2. Discuss 3rd writing project (In Retrospect) and the elements it will contain:
    -Back story of writer (minus details of particular crime and victims names).
    -No glorifying past or self gratification.
    -No rationalizing criminal behavior, excuse making, or blaming others, including society.
    -However, events and experiences that steered you the wrong way are permissible
    -Further, talk about what events/experiences put you on the path to change your life and how you plan to remain crime free and live a victimless life, both while in prison and when/if paroled. Remember: The esence of the message is "If I knew then what I know now" things would have been different, my actions would have been ndifferent.
    -Writing is to be 3-5 pages long and legible.

Project Overview
Week 5

1. Pledge recited.
2. Book of stamps required from each participant.
3. Review of copyright and publishing material.

Project Overview
Week 6

1. Pledge recited.
2. Submission of victims impact letter for review and discussion.

Project Overview
Week 7

1. Pledge recited.
2. Review and evaluate progress on "In Retrospect" writing.

Project Overview
Week 8

1. Pledge recited
2. Victims impact discussion

Note:

The remaining classes will be for proof reading, editing, and preparing work

product for publishing.

Epilogue

It is with great pride that I observe the work being done by these gentlemen in the <u>Write Our Wrongs</u> program. Not only am I proud to see that they are making attempts to begin the healing process and reconcile with the victims of their crimes, but I am equally proud that they are doing this healing and reconciliation within themselves. We are all human beings on our own personal journeys, and all deserving of grace. This program and the curriculums associated with it are, in my opinion, part of the important internal work that we ALL must do when coming to grips with the times in our lives when we have fallen short.

There was a period in my life when my friends, many of whom shared the same upbringing as myself, began to go to prison, some for long periods of time. I began to wonder what was different about their lives that caused them to make the choices that ultimately led to their incarceration. However, as a person free in the world, I quickly allowed this contemplation to dissipate, and went on with my life. Those individuals did not have this luxury. Many spent years thinking about the events that caused their incarceration and their willing participation in such events. Some of these individuals fell further, choosing not to heal, grow and arise better from their circumstances. They wallowed in their misery and stayed in that miserable place, many even after gaining freedom. But others, those who chose to truly explore their choices and the consequences of their actions, moved down the arduous path toward healing, eventually being able to become productive citizens, mentors, fathers, brothers and sons - whether or not they gained their physical freedom.

It is the redemption of this second group that is the focus of the Write Our Wrongs program. And it is through structure, scholarship and brotherhood that they achieve this goal. The fact that this is a prisoner- initiated and administered program should not be overlooked, as it signifies that these are people who are not waiting to "be rehabilitated," they are making tangible strides to rehabilitate themselves, and perhaps be able to help in the healing process for the victims of their crimes as well. This is humanity at its BEST.

-- Tajai Massey

CPSIA information can be obtained
at www.ICGtesting.com
Printed in the USA
LVHW102036151220
674112LV00012B/321